GLACIER'S SECRETS

Volume II

Goat Trails and Grizzly Tales

by GEORGE OSTROM
with the Over-the-Hill Gang

FARCOUNTRY PRESS

Left: WINTER ON CLEMENTS—As the snow moves in there are three things wildlife can do: 1. Sleep a few months in a den or burrow; 2. Go someplace else; 3. Stay right here and tough it out. After this fourteen-mile hike up the Garden Wall, Bob Zavadil chose number 2.

Facing page: A TRAIL GOES UP— Swiftcurrent Pass is switchbacks over Continental Divide through cliffs, below glaciers, and waterfalls. Looking over Bullhead Lake, pink things are spiraea. Take away the scenery and what have you got? North Dakota.

Page 1: COUNT THE COLORS— Imagine a thousand acres of constantly changing wild flowers and you have Preston Park from June through August. This July photo was taken near junction of trails to Siyeh Pass and Peigan Pass. First blooms of season are glacier lilies by the zillions. Griz dig and eat the roots which, by the way, are very tasty.

Front cover: ON TOP OF THE LITTLE MATTERHORN, Ivan O'Neil surveys the vastness of Glacier National Park. Four thousand feet below is Avalanche Lake, and on down the canyon is a short stretch of Going-to the-Sun Road where visitors can glimpse this pyramid-shaped mountain. I know of no one who has climbed to more high places in Glacier than Ivan. It is genetic. His grandmother, Freida O'Neil, was the first woman to climb the remote Grinnell Mountain in 1903.

Back cover: "AN AWESOME COULOIR"—That's what Edwards calls this spectacular spot. The exposure is great but goat ledge is wider here than in other places. I yelled at daughter Heidi to wait on that point because there is a bad spot just beyond…the ledge ends.

ISBN (softcover): 1-56037-166-8
ISBN (hardcover): 1-56037-173-0
© 2000 Farcountry Press/Montana Magazine
Text and photography © 2000 G. George Ostrom

This book is dedicated to my daughters Heidi and Wendy, their husbands Scott and Shawn. Add their kids Tana, Parker, Wyatt, and special thoughts for daughter-in-law Michele Nielsen Ostrom. There's a big box of hearty handshakes in here for the Over-the-Hill Gang, with whom I've shared so many unforgettable times. Love you all.

INTRODUCTION

Doing a book like Glacier's Secrets, and this Volume II, is a fun frustration. Book signings, slide shows, and talks with folks along the trail, constantly remind me, each photo triggers curiosity about related wonders.

"George, you talk of Ptarmigan Tunnel coming out on the face of giant cliffs but you don't show us."

"Your book mentions 'The Great Cleft' on Mt. Pollack. Couldn't you have had it in there?"

"The Matterhorn is described as a precipitous horn far from anyplace. People would like to see that."

The book has not been done that does full honor to Glacier's vastness, and it never will be. That's part of the intrigue. People like me can only tantalize and inspire others to explore and protect this special place.

Volume II has more "how we went" sequences of favorite climbs on known and obscure peaks, along with the inspiring panoramas revealed. Included are road and trail vistas many visitors miss. The accent is on wilderness adventures that can be done in one day, then cherished for a lifetime.

Volume II is not a "Look, don't touch" scenery album. You are up there with us regular people…enjoying magnificence.

Come along , share with us…

Right: PRESTON PARK PARADISE— Surrounded by lofty crags, laced by ponds, crystal streams, and hundreds of plant varieties, this alpine garden-park is visited by bighorns, elk, deer, goats, little critters, and grizzly bears. Gang is looking things over from southeast ridge of Siyeh. To southwest are peaks from Logan Pass to Sperry Glacier and at right is Piegan Mountain and Glacier. Preston Park is moderate uphill walk of two and a half miles from Siyeh Bend off Going-to-the-Sun Road.

FLINSCH PEAK IN FALL—Trail west here goes to Old Man Lake, over Pitamakan Pass to Cutbank Pass, then south to Dawson Pass. From there it is a short climb up Flinsch from the far side. Got above trail to take this photo so there'd be full color in foreground. Youngman and Boy Lakes occupy shelves on Flinsch, with only goat trails reaching them.

PREFACE

This book is pure "show and tell," photos and stories of enthusiastic people exploring America's most diverse national park, ranging from lowland fern and cedar forests up to high arctic climes of perpetual snow and ice. The magic is in exotic plants, twisted geology, and the unbelievable wildlife each level reveals.

The Thursday Over-the-Hill Gang has racked up another thousand miles on trails, goat ledges, and high peaks in Glacier since George's first book in early 1997. That's a hundred more days in wonderland. Two more members have gone to the big alpine meadow in the sky and the core group is getting older than dirt. The good news is younger people are joining the Thursday climbs and the average age is dropping.

They've seen more grizzlies. That is why there are more photos and tales about America's largest carnivore. While the big bears are a threatened symbol of wilderness, they also present a very real danger to humans.

Ostrom says, "Adventuring within pristine wilderness has always been an act of joy and wonder, but perhaps the richest reward comes from reliving and sharing memorable days with those who couldn't be with us."

The Over-the-Hill Gang, who've chosen to climb year-round in Glacier, do not just see places visited by few, but are in the park when first spring flowers valiantly push their heads through receding snow. The gang revels in the rainbow bloomings of summer and the dazzling foliage of fall. They are also there as the curtain falls…when the great storms of winter cover it all in deep cold white.

That's what this book is about.

GLACIER LILIES—Called these dogtooth violets when I was a boy. They are so eager to get going in the spring, they come right up through the snow. Took photo in Hanging Gardens at Logan Pass, where they turn their world bright yellow.

Above: IN THE CLOUDS—Ivan and I spent an hour atop Swiftcurrent Mountain in a complete white-out. Just as we started down the clouds moved away, revealing the magnificent Swiftcurrent Valley and towering peaks that line each side. There was an outhouse near the look-out tower, held to the cliff top by steel cables anchored in rocks, but it blew away. Two years later on an AMTRAK trip to Minot, North Dakota, we spotted what appeared to be the outhouse a hundred miles out on the plains…still attached to the rocks. The wind really blows up there.

Right: GEORGE ON THE TOILET—I'm glad I wasn't standing there when the thing blew away. *(Ivan O'Neil photo)*

Facing page: HALF WAY UP—A thousand feet above Swiftcurrent Lake, Dean and Bob said this is easy. Told 'em, "The last half is steeper, but there is water on the south face ascent."

GOING TO KUPUNKAMINT—The trail along Cutbank Creek is a garden in summer. After we'd climbed most peaks here, I suggested Kupunkamint but nobody had heard of it. Walter Bahr led a successful climb, with most getting torn clothes and lacerated bodies; however six of us "candy fannies" quit when the going got tough. Kupunkamint means "Shakes Himself" in Kootenai.

THREE BABY BEARS—Triplet black bears are not unusual. These are still nursing while learning other food sources; however, they were playing here while mother dug roots. Good numbers of black bears in Glacier. Some have to be killed after thoughtless visitors turn them to dangerous beggers with handouts. Posters say, "A fed bear is a dead bear."

SHOOTING STARS—
If there is no such thing
as albino plants, then
two here are genetically
confused. Violet is the
color of choice for these
hardy beauties. When
my son Shannon was
small he told me,
"Shooting Stars smell
purple."

NOTHIN' TO IT—Young Pat Galvin seems to be wishing he'd never gone with his dad's weird friends to climb Wolverine Point. Dean Dahlgren is explaining, "Heck, that little crack's nothin'. I made it and I only have one arm." Pat said, "Yeah, but you've got experienced shoes." We all made it.

Facing page: A RAINBOW SURPRISE—Closeup of St. Mary Falls. No one knows for sure how many waterfalls are in Glacier Park but some, like this one, are well known because they're easy to reach. George Tolman fishes here but doesn't catch any.

ONE LOOK SAYS GRIZZLY—The bear down there is not a huge speci-
men but it looks one hundred percent griz, distinctive hump, dished face,
power-packed muscles. A walking grizzly isn't poetry in motion, but it can
move fast. There is majesty to their bearing...mystery in their presence.

Facing page: NOT TODAY—One of the Gang stands in the pass between
Reynolds and the Dragon's Tail studying our climbing route up The Tail.
A hike to this point requires no climbing and presents outstanding views
of the Twin Lakes cirque and many mountains of The Crown. To the west
are Gunsight Mountain and Sperry Glacier.

Above: WHITE BOG ORCHID—
The Danny On flower book says this
plant has a "striking fragrance." We
know it smells good. Have never
counted exactly but there are near
fifty tiny orchids on one main stem.
See them in wet places. This one near
Many Glacier entrance, July 8.

Right: WATCHING A MOOSE—
He is more than a mile away but Bob
looks back to check on a bull moose
we met down there near the trail. It's
feeding in Bullhead Lake. Red-col-
ored mountain in eastern distance is
Altyn, at right Grinnell. Swiftcurrent
Pass is an excellent "cross-over" hike.
Traded car keys with members coming over from Sun Road. We started
at Swiftcurrent Trailhead.

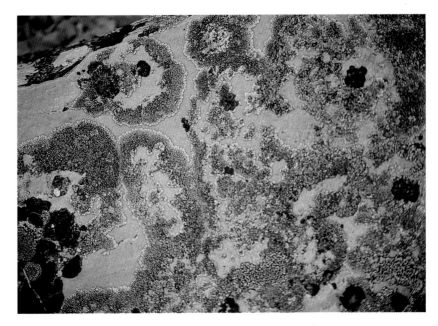

Above: GREEN LICHENS AT WORK—Lichens are slow workers. Their job is eating rocks and that takes time because they do it by manufacturing chemicals. Scientists say certain lichens only grow half an inch in a thousand years. I'll come back to check these, then let you know.

Left: ASPEN AT TWO DOG FLAT—This area has the greatest concentration of Glacier's elk. Aspen trees brighten up scenery in September and October. Mountain is Single Shot, where I once broke four ribs. Fell while dodging a falling rock. Gang got in debate about who got to go for help and who had to stay. Jack was winning because he had my extra car key. I settled the argument by walking out. Tried not to laugh a lot.

Left: TANA VISITS OBERLIN—Bought Heidi's daughter, Tana, a little backpack for her first hike with Grandpa when she was three but she made me carry it. Got to a waterfall for lunch and discovered I'd left mine in the car. She gave me the crusts from her sandwich. On way down she picked a flower for her mother so we had "the flower talk." Tana agreed she'd leave all the flowers for other little kids, but she was going to sit on some.

Below: BOB IN BEARGRASS—Trail to Apikuni Falls, late July. We dawdled but still managed to climb 4,200 vertical to Apikuni summit. Saw sheep, goats, and one scraggly bear.

Facing page: VIRGINIA FALLS—Ed Maul stands tall. Told him to assume his "in awe" pose. This wonderful water display is easily reachable from Going-to-the-Sun Road on trail. Going there from Sunrift Gorge is a couple of miles and gives you three major falls plus unnamed cascades along the way.

Three Consecutive Thursdays

July 17, 1998, the Pinnacle Wall Goat Trail

Fantastic is a good word for this short version of Dr. Edwards' famous Ptarmigan-Tunnel-to-Ahern-Pass-wall walk. (J. Gordon Edwards' *A Climber's Guide to Glacier National Park* is a classic.) It is five miles up to the tunnel from Swiftcurrent trailhead, a wonderful trip on its own. This day we did the first mile of ledge, then climbed the north side, played on top, then descended what was for us a new route down the south wall. Total distance was 12 miles, maybe the greatest 12 miles in America.

NORTH EXIT—Tunnel is black dot in middle. Still snow where sun never shines. This view illustrates where trail had to be blasted from solid rock. Completion made a needed shortcut between Many Glacier and Belly River.

THE WALK BEGINS—First section of goat trail reached by getting on top of the wall directly above Ptarmigan Tunnel. The gang knows about two thousand feet of nothing on their right...but views are worth the scare.

NORTH PORTAL OF PTARMIGAN TUNNEL—Heavy doors are
shut in fall to keep wind from packing tunnel full of snow. The tunnel
was completed in 1931 by workers who hung perilously from ropes
anchored into the cliffs.

LOOKING TOWARDS CANADA—Over-the-Hill Gang at north portal. Gene is showing Walt the best ledge not to walk on.

Facing page: HELEN LAKE—Waterfalls feed this lofty emerald jewel from Ahern Peak and Ahern Glacier then flow to Hudson Bay, three thousand miles away. I believe the lake was named after the eldest daughter of fur trader Malcomb Clark and his second wife, a Piegan woman named Kakokima. The best source on these matters is *Place Names of Glacier/Waterton National Parks* by Jack Holterman.

WALL WALKERS—Kristen Shwartz and Heidi Duncan pause to revel in views from the goat ledge on north side of Ptarmigan Wall. Here's where adventuresome hikers get first glimpses of entrancing Helen Lake.

Facing page: "AN AWESOME COULOIR"—That's what Edwards calls this spectacular spot. The exposure is great but goat ledge is wider here than in other places. I yelled at daughter Heidi to wait on that point because there is a bad spot just beyond…the ledge ends.

DOWN FROM THE WALL—Over-the-Hill Gang members pose on trail back to
Swiftcurrent with our Pinnacle Wall in distance. Descent of south side was easier than it
looks. Low place at right is area of Ptarmigan Tunnel.

Facing page: ATOP THE PINNACLE WALL—Kristen Shwartz studies the trail where we
came up that morning. A switchback to Ptarmigan Tunnel is visible as is the trail into the
south portal. She's near base of the "Great Ptarmigan Spire." This day we descended the
south wall rather than continue to Ahern Pass. Far ridge leads to Crowfeet Mountain.

July 24th: Bishops Cap and Pollock

ED DAWDLING—On Highline Trail from Logan Pass. People like Ed Maul get delayed by ogling the wild petunias.

Facing page: GOAL FROM AFAR—Bishops Cap is a distinctive part of the Continental Divide. View here is from a ridge southwest of Logan Pass. Bighorn ram had a bad leg, a dangerous thing because a mountain lion was in this area.

Right: GOLDEN MANTLE CHIPMUNK—This little fellow was greeting hikers on the Sperry Glacier Trail. Naturally shy, they live in the rocks, mostly near timberline. When fed, they can become real pests. At Cobalt Lake, one of them sneaked inside my backpack and nibbled a trail snack.

Below: These exquisite plants grow in rocks. Don't know their name. Flower book writers may have missed them. With over a thousand species of vascular plants in Glacier, that could happen. Glowing arrangement was on south face of Otokomi at 7,000 feet in June.

Facing page: JULIE'S FIRST CLIMB—When we headed up the Garden Wall off the Highline trail, Julie Greiner said she couldn't see a path. Friend Heidi told her, "These old guys find their own." Halfway up from the Trail to the rugged crest between Bishops Cap and Pollock Mountain.

WINGED PREDATOR—Glacier is home to many hunting birds, including owls, golden eagles, bald eagles, and hawks. Redtail hawks like this one are seen on the eastern front. Songbirds are numerous, including mountain bluebirds along with jays, ducks, and trumpeter swans.

Facing page: THE GREAT DIVIDE—Ray Kenney strolls the Continental Divide between Bishops Cap and Pollock. Sheer cliffs to his left drop thousands of feet into Cataract Creek. Nobody we know climbs that side.

DOING THE CONTINENTAL—
Looking north up the Divide
toward Bishops Cap as we near top
of Pollock. Mountain in center is
Gould.

FRIENDS IN HIGH PLACES—Nine Over-the-Hillers on top Bishops Cap at one time. Well! Somebody had to stay at the bottom and take the pictures.

RED BUSHES—Do not know species of this October subject. The Park is full of this particular berry plant, but four educated people I asked said, "They're red bushes."

IMPORTANT RITUAL—"We claim this mountain and all lands where its waters flow, in the name of the United States of America." Have done this on a lot of peaks over the last forty years. Here on Pollock, the claimed area takes in a huge hunk of Canada. Lucky we keep good records. (*Julie Greiner photo*)

STUDYING THE CROWN—Major peaks from left to right include Blackfoot, Heavy Runner (left foreground), Jackson, Citadel, Reynolds, Gunsight (distance), Dragons Tail, Edwards, Little Matterhorn, Bear Hat, Brown, and bit of Clements. Oberlin Bend on Going-to-the-Sun Road lower right and Lunch Creek Bend straight down. Logan Pass is hidden by Pollock's south buttress.

HAPPY BIRTHDAY—Julie, Heidi, and Elmer laughed when wind blew George's candle out. Blew Julie's party hat away too. Otherwise, it was a good 69th birthday party.

THE GREAT CLEFT—Nature created a crack in the cliff making a natural climbing route on south face of Pollock. Heidi waits at the upper entrance while Ed, Ray, Bob and Julie fingernail their way down.

ALPINE ESCALATOR—Other routes down Pollock's summit cliffs take an hour longer. While putting pressure against walls with your arms there is a feeling of security. Too bad there aren't more "Great Clefts" in Glacier.

Facing page: "GOING DOWN?"—The Great Cleft is not wide but portly members have done it. Mountain in distance is Cannon, and farther to the right is McPartland in the Livingston Range.

July 31st: Bear Hat

The toughest part of doing Bear Hat is climbing back up from Hidden Lake on the return trip. It is four miles from Logan pass to the point where we start up this unique pyramid of rock. Total vertical is over 3,000 feet and distance ten miles with every step providing beauty and adventure.

THERE ARE THE CARS— Telephoto shot from the lower entrance of the Cleft shows vehicles on Sun Road at Lunch Creek. Station wagon with the white top contains ice cold "refreshments," but there are still a few lesser cliffs to deal with. Saw band of bighorn rams, marmots, and one wolverine on descent, also many flowers.

CUTTHROAT IN CREEK—The Hidden Lake outlet is one of the most frigid crossings I know, even in late July, but it is on the way to Bearhat. We waded it in June once, before we knew better, and one guy was so chilled, he got slush on his bladder. This photo shows cutthroat spawning. The outlet area is closed to fishing and watched by eagle-eyed rangers.

WOLF AND OWL?—I honestly don't know if these are lupine and owl clover or not. The book says there are 600 species of lupine, from the Latin, *lupus*, wolf. Early botanists thought it robbed the soil. Book says it adds nitrogen. If these aren't owl clover and lupine, they should be.

CLIFFED OUT—Couldn't keep climbing this nice couloir, gully to flat landers, because it ended in a cliff, so Heidi went scouting for another route. We'd had lunch on the edge of that snow field below and were anxious to get on top.

Left: "WE WERE THERE"—From the summit ridge of Bearhat, Heidi shows Julie last Thursday's mountains, Bishops Caps and Pollock. Nearer peak is Clements just west of Logan Pass. Pollock's top is shaped like a mesa and The Great Cleft is a bit left of center in those cliffs. We performed the claiming ritual on top of Bearhat and walked back to Logan Pass before dark, midst the goats, deer, and a faraway griz.

Below: GOAL FOR TODAY—Bearhat Mountain stands just west of Hidden Lake and the Continental Divide. Its central location gives views to most of the mountains in Glacier Park. More snow than usual forced us to go farther around the south side before starting our climb, but we still had to cross several large snow fields where ice axes were handy.

HAVE TO LOOK QUICK—Approaching Avalanche from the east along McDonald Creek, a glance to the south gives peek at the Little Matterhorn. Telephoto shot from the road also shows the taller Edwards Mountain beyond.

Left: A GOOD ANGLE—The exquisite Hidden Lake brings awe to thousands who hike the boardwalk from Logan Pass to the Overlook each summer. A loftier view is available from the Dragon's Tail. Daughter Wendy and son Clark went with me to attempt Mount Cannon years ago, but the area was closed by a sign warning of grizzly bears so we did this instead. *(Wendy or Clark Ostrom photo)*

Below: VIEW FROM CLIFF TOPS— Glacial silt adds special blue-green color to high lakes in the park. Avalanche is a good example.

About Grizzlies

Grizzly bears have always been part of Glacier. In the park's early days the big bears were hunted, as a policy. Indian history written by James Willard Schultz details chilling human encounters with the aggressive animals before whites came.. These mainly occurred on the eastern side.

I recall as a boy in the 1930s going to Many Glacier Hotel and seeing dozens of grizzly rugs decorating balcony railings in the big lobby. As late as the fifties and sixties it was rare to see a live one.

Local people and the park administration were shocked when two young women were attacked and killed on the same night in August 1967, at two separate areas: Granite Park and Trout Lake. "The Night of the Grizzlies" was a wakeup call. I covered those tragic events for Time-Life and am the only reporter to go to scenes of all fatalities since then. The Park Service officially recognized only ten human deaths because they have no physical proof in the 1997 hiker disappearance at Two Medicine, but the veteran rangers know. The female responsible was destroyed along with her two large cubs after they killed and ate another lone hiker there in 1998.

When the Endangered Species Act brought federal protective action, the big bears began a comeback and management problems arose. Today there is an educated estimate of four to five hundred grizzlies in and around Glacier Park. We see them often. Many members of the Over-the-Hill Gang used to carry big caliber handguns illegally, with the thought we did not want to curl up and play dead while a grizzly killed one of our friends or family. My .357 magnum was in a camera case labeled "Cannon." Not entirely deceitful.

In the early nineties we developed faith in the powerful pepper sprays and now carry holstered canisters. I've interviewed over twenty people who stopped charging bears with the spray, and am not aware of any incident where it was properly used and failed to save the victim.

Current Park Service policy is to close trails frequented by grizzlies and use "adverse conditioning" on those near people places. Many bears have been captured and transplanted but that doesn't work well and bears have to be killed. Adverse conditioning by harassing them with Kerilian bear dogs while firing rubber bullets and cracker shells seems to be working on some grizzlies.

Grizzly bears are amazing, interesting, and magnificent creatures to observe. They are awkward to deal with politically because they are higher up on the food chain than we are. Who wants to eat one anyway?

CLOSE UP AND PERSONAL—Male grizzly had approached hikers at Red Rock Lake and one visitor fired shots over his head. An investigation followed and the shooter was cited. There is a fine for carrying guns in Glacier, more if you shoot. This is the same bear standing up on cover of our book *Wondrous Wildlife*.

"BEAR VALLEY" DOWN THERE—Maps list that valley as Granite Park. It's a lush area with ponds and streams and lies immediately south of Granite Park Chalet. Our record August sighting of grizzlies there was seven at one time. Telescopes at the chalet let visitors study the bears at a safe distance.

THE MIGHTY JACKSON—Heidi and Grace Guest sat down for the "claiming ritual" on Lincoln Peak above Sperry Chalet, so they wouldn't block view of Lake Ellen Wilson and Mount Jackson. Jackson is one of six Glacier peaks over 10,000 feet and dominates this area. Wide-angle lens makes it look smaller than it is. Hike to Lincoln Peak is eight miles by trail and 4,000 feet vertical. Well worth it.

EAST FACE OF JACKSON—Don't understand how but here are still glaciers hanging on the south face of that mighty mountain. Jackson is the peak seen by George Bird Grinnell in 1891 which inspired him to call Glacier "The Crown of the Continent." A great hike goes along the north side up to Gunsight Pass, best done in late summer or early fall.

WHERE WE LOST A FRIEND—An Over-the-Hill member fell from a goat trail high on these Stoney Indian Peaks in September of 1998. Roger Dokken was returning from a successful ascent of Glacier's highest point, Mount Cleveland, when he fell over a thousand feet into the canyon. Marvin Parker just ahead of him heard no sound until Roger's body hit a ledge. The Park Service lists his death as "a climber fall," but most of us feel something physical happened, because of his silence. Flew over with Mike Strand and Charlie Bleck after the accident. Snow wasn't here when Roger fell.

RESCUE RANGERS—Saving injured climbers and recovering bodies can be a technical operation in high, rough terrain. Glacier trains and maintains a core group of rangers for that demanding work. In this practice exercise the "volunteer victim" happened to be a comely young woman. They had her out in forty-five minutes. I asked the leader, "How long would it take if the victim was a grandpa?" He only smiled.

CUTTHROAT SUPPER—The rare flyfishing we do is mostly "catch and release" but these were carried out for a baked trout feast. Ranger son Shannon caught them while eleven guys yelled conflicting tips on how to land 'em. Many lakes in Glacier are home to trout and angling is regulated so generations to come can enjoy this wonderful experience.

Facing page: CREEKS WITH NO NAMES—All along McDonald Creek are feeder streams coming off Stanton, Vaught, McPartland, and Heavens peaks. This is one in October. Avalanches are frequent here during winter then grizzlies gather on the fans in spring, looking for animals killed by snowslides.

WHERE A GRIZZLY DUG—Hi Gibson said, "Jack! Don't poke in that hole." Jack replied, "Well, if there's a bear there it can't be very big." Bears excavated to get gophers and marmots. They have some success or they wouldn't keep doing it.

SILVERTIP DIGGER—Grizzly bears claw up acres and acres of glacier lily and other roots. Theory is, they developed distinctive hump on the shoulders by all this digging through hundreds of generations.

Facing page: LAKE PITAMAKAN—Bob Z. said, "Looks Steep," from the pass to the lake. To Bob's left is Lake of the Seven Winds, and others are down toward Cutbank Ranger Station, Katoya and Morning Star. Big Peak to north is Medicine Grizzly. Mile west is Cutbank Pass where spectacular trail goes along Continental Divide to Dawson Pass and back down to Two Medicine. One of the best "loops" in this Park. I say it's twenty miles, but people with long legs say it's eighteen.

"CURLY BEAR"—That's what they call that mountain of jumbled rock at the left. From the top of Divide Mountain the whole world looks a little jumbled, the result of a horrendous split in the earth's surface millions of years ago. View is west up St. Mary valley toward Logan Pass. Mountain on right is Going to the Sun. On this day, most of the gang climbed a peak south of Curly Bear called White Calf and some of them got cliffed out so didn't get to the top. They saw bears.

NORTHERN LIVINGSTON RANGE—Readers of my books and newspaper columns
ask if the Over-the-Hill Gang hikes and climbs in this remote part of Glacier. The
answer is "a little." Most of the peaks just south of the Canadian border cannot be
done in one day, especially by overly mature people. Some of us have done the trails
but not climbed a lot. Shown here are Lakes Wurdeman and Nooney two miles north
of Brown Pass and below Hudson Glacier. Two big peaks at right center are Kintla and
Kinnerly. Bobbi Gilmore, who climbs with us, did Kintla in mid 1990s and her crew
was hounded by grizzlies much of the time. If you can get good grizzly photos without
a telephoto lens, I don't want to go.

YUM YUM—If any wild fruit taste better than huckleberries off the bush I don't know about it. Ate 'em all in one bite. Good huckleberry years are best for everyone because bears get fat without raiding people places.

BOB IN BALSAM—A June hike to Swiftcurrent Ridge from Many Glacier entrance station reveals flowers galore, also bears: five blacks and one grizzly. Almost saw a moose.

BENEATH THE SUMMIT CLIFFS—A "viewtiful" goat trail traverses southward around the east wall of Grinnell Point but it's no place for handsprings.
Long ways down.

LIGHTED LARCH—Sun makes them glow. Not all change color at once. McDonald Valley and Middle Fork of the Flathead are two places to see this fall phenomenon.

PARKER AND THE POSIES—Parker went on his first hike at three. We did the waterfall trail at St. Mary Lake and he wanted to run. Explained, "In the park we go slowly and smell the flowers." He decided to smell every one of 'em. Took half an hour to go a hundred feet. Parker is Tana's little brother. Dad is Scott Duncan.

DREAMING OF SIYEH—From a sharp spire on Cracker Peak, Bob Z said he wanted to someday climb the mighty Siyeh, and his wish came true. Trouble was, when The Gang reached the over-10,000-foot summit, fog was so thick they couldn't see fifty feet. Didn't bother Ed Maul and me…we turned back half way up in the clouds. Sights from top of Siyeh include a scary peek 4,000 feet down to Cracker Lake. Maybe next time, Bob.

DUMBEST OR BRAVEST?—A grizzly is digging in a gopher hole beside the trail to Apikuni Falls. One hundred feet away another gopher is standing up just asking for attention. Merely foolish.

WHAT SIGN IS THIS?—Park pamphlets say hikers should wear little bells in the back country to let grizzlies know they are coming. Helps prevent "surprise encounters." Literature also says there are two kinds of bears—blacks and grizzly—and you can tell if any are around by studying droppings. Some say griz poo-poo has bells in it. Every book should include a little humor.

THE CROWN IS WHITE—Big peaks around Logan Pass on the Continental Divide in late November. The pass is just left of center. Horn in middle is Reynolds. When seen like this it seems impossible in seven months those mountains will be alive with wild creatures, green grass, and dainty flowers. The world is full of miraculous things, many of them right here.

Facing page: NOT MUCH FROM HERE—The Little Matterhorn looks kinda puny up there between Mounts Brown and Edwards, but that is deceiving. Our hike-climb from this west side, then returning to McDonald via Sperry glacier, involved over 5,000 vertical feet and eighteen miles. October panorama is from shore of Lake McDonald where turning larch provides a golden touch.

Left: GLACIER WALKER—Ed is not alone, George is behind. Exit off this icy western arm of Sperry Glacier is tricky. It's a long slippery slide to make shortcut over to Comeau Pass. Mountain is Edwards. It had been a long day, car still ten miles away. Ed wanted to know if we were still having fun.

Below: HIGH COUNTRY HOTEL—Granite Park Chalet sits on the Garden Wall overlooking the Livingston Range and some spectacular parts of the Lewis Range. We like it so much we even go up when it's closed.

Facing page: DRINKING SNOW— On a sunny day climb of Clements west ridge, Ivan found a bit of snow. Said he was going to hold the cup until it melted enough for a drink. Pat Gyrion waved and yelled for us to wait up. I hollered, "Take yer time! We're gonna to be here two hours."

A GRIZZLY ENCOUNTER

Above: HIKERS SEE GRIZZLY—August 13, 1998. The Gang retreated toward Granite Park Chalet when this griz came out of brush below the trail. Watched him feed easterly through the meadow. We yelled at hikers on the Highline Trail to be careful and not come farther. In half an hour there were a dozen hikers in trees over there. One fellow whom we'd met earlier and named "Motorcycle Guy," tried to sneak over where we were and the bear made a bluff jump at him. Motorcycle Guy sneaked back.

Right: BACK OFF—Grizzlies seem to have a tolerance zone. If you're beyond it they ignore you but if you get too close they may charge. Trouble is the zone varies from bear to bear and time to time. We knew where this guy's zone was when he looked at us. This color phase is called silvertip.

74

Below: TIME FOR ACTION—As time wore on in this confrontation, I was becoming worried about too many people gathering around the bear. I yelled suggestions to some, and a tourist asked, "Is that guy a ranger?" Jack said he was leaving because he was out of film. I handed him a new roll so he had to stay with me, but other OTHG members took my car key and headed out for the Loop.

Was mighty glad to see "Bear Ranger" Brian McKeon arrive. Unknown to us, someone had radioed out earlier that a grizzly was near the trail and Brian had run that steep four miles from Sun Road. His uniform was soaking wet. He asked everyone to move farther back from the bear, then loaded a twelve-gauge shotgun to shoot a rubber projectile, followed with a booming cracker shell. He told us this bear had already been given the treatment twice. Must have a tough hindy.

In the photo Ranger McKeon is ready to shoot the bear in the butt with the bouncy bullet. Some hikers can be seen across the meadow in the trees. More were behind me. It was a tense time because one can never be positive how an alarmed grizzly will react. I assumed McKeon had "real" backup slugs in the magazine.

Brian fired the harassing shots. The griz jumped, then ran the way he's facing, northeast. Hiker traffic resumed. A thing that concerned McKeon was, the trail to Swiftcurrent Pass comes in from the northeast and the bear might tangle with hikers up there, so he went to check.

Everyone was talking at once. A lady hiker near me loudly expressed outrage at the ranger's "cruel treatment of an innocent animal." Told her the ranger might have

just saved a human life, as well as the bear's. Couldn't help adding, "Thirty-one years ago I was sitting right here beside one dead grizzly and three more were just beyond the chalet. The bodies of two young women were lying in a Kalispell mortuary, and this beautiful place was filled with grieving. I'm sorry, ma'am, but there is a great deal you do not know about grizzly bears and people."

MANY GLACIER HOTEL—A national treasure, the hotel and surroundings on Swiftcurrent Lake are a beautiful sight from top of Grinnell Point. People are loading on the boat. 300 MM telephoto shot.

Facing page: SOMEONE'S ON TOP—While climbing Oberlin, Heidi spots an Over-the-Hiller topping out Clements. Four of them went up the vertical front. Can't see him? Maybe you could use a magnifying glass.

THE EYES OF WILDERNESS—
Wolves moved back to ancestral lands
in Glacier years ago from Canada but
have ups and downs getting established.
Numbers have varied from dozens
down to less than ten at times. North
Fork of the Flathead is where they've
done best because of prey populations
of deer and elk.

WOLF TRACK—Wolves have big feet. This
imprint near packers Roost is five-and-one-
half inches long. Large pads enable wolves to
travel well in snow. They are an amazing,
complex, beautiful animal, but I've seen
guys eating a hamburger call them cold-
blooded killers. Point of view is a relative
matter.

Facing Page: BENT ROCKS—When you are 6,500 feet above sea level, it is difficult to imagine those lay-
ers of rock being formed by water, but that's what the geologists say. Many wonders can be seen on this
hike over 7,750-foot Siyeh Pass. Wind turned very cold near the top just as camera batteries lost power.
Do not believe anyone who tells you batteries regain power if you warm them in your jockey shorts.

Right: SO MUCH FOR SIGNS—Common sight in the backcountry are remains of trail signs that displeased a passing grizzly. The bear that "swiped out" this one, thoughtfully left half. Claw marks in the post resemble chainsaw cuts. That's a little scary. New signs are steel but they still get bashed.

Below: A MAJESTIC STAG—Wild bull elk are hard to photograph in Glacier. Three of us spent hours getting close to one in fall of '99. He had a large harem. Ladies didn't want to lose lover boy so one or more cows were always alert to danger. Good place to see elk is near St. Mary Lake on Two Dog Flats, evening and early morning.

Facing page: AUTUMN ON ALDER TRAIL—The park abandoned Alder Trail after the "Night of the Grizzlies" in August 1967, when a young woman was killed at Granite Park Chalet. The route goes up from Sun Road and hits Highline Trail near the chalet, but passes too close to "Bear Valley." We started up in '98 but it's a shin-tangle.

Right: PLEASE PASS THE CHAINSAW—
We don't ask anyone over seventy-five to
run power saws. That's why Elmer has a
shovel. Cleared over six miles of the Ole
Creek Trail. When there are more trees
across we don't get that far in one day.

Below: THE GANG'S ALL HERE—
Majority of the hardcore Thursday Over-
the-Hill Gang showed up at Walton Ranger
Station to clear Ole Creek Trail in May
1997. Average age here is over 65. Founder,
Ambrose Measure, at far right, was eighty-
nine. We try to give something back to the
park that gives us so much.

Facing page: ALL DOWN HILL NOW—
After clearing Swiftcurrent Pass, the trail
drops down to Granite Park Chalet. Millions
of glacier lilies were in bloom. Far beyond
the chalet is Heavens Peak in the Livingston
Range. Ray was keeping a sharp eye out for
grizzlies. Lot of 'em in this area.

LATE SEPTEMBER—Many flowers tough it out through the first frosts but there are not many left by the end of September. That's when a whole new world of color explodes in Glacier. The Gang is headed toward Old Man Lake out of Two Medicine. Saw no other hikers but much wildlife.

Above: A GOOD SUNSET—Took this across Lake McDonald looking over Howe Ridge on drive home from Bishops Cap climb. Standard sunset in Glacier can be a religious experience.

Right: AFTER A FIRE STORM—Nine years following the Red Bench fire in lodgepole stands near Polebridge, the remaining black snags were still falling to nourish the next forest. Right after that September fire, new vegetation popped up through the ashes. Some seeds lie dormant for decades until opened by wildfire. That's the way it works.

THE RAMS AT MANY GLACIER—There are several winter ranges where bighorns band together to survive the months of snow. Biggest one in Glacier is on Mounts Altyn and Henkel. We see up to sixty rams at one time in May. Sheep scatter into high country for summer, rams separate from ewes and lambs. People who move slowly, avoid eye contact, and don't walk directly at them can get close. Jack just sits down.

WOLF VERSUS SHEEP—Ray Kenney talked me into walking eight miles into Many Glacier before the road opened in April 1999. Offered to pack my heavy 400 MM telephoto. He spotted a wolf. Using binocs we watched it pick up scent of a small band of bighorns feeding above this snow field.

The wolf worked closer staying downwind until the sheep spotted him, then he charged full out. The pursuit went toward another snow-field and we figured he would catch one when they hit that, but the sheep went around the deep stuff then full tilt up cliffs. The wolf was either young or famished because when it hit the cliffs it tried to go up, too. Momentum helped carry him fifteen or twenty feet high but he lost footing and fell back to the base, hitting heavily. It was enough to end his plans. Couldn't help admire the bighorns' skill, but sort of felt sorry for the wolf.

THIS IS IT—In the first *Glacier's Secrets* book I told of our frustrating search for a "scenic route" to Otokomi Lake, walking the precipitous ridge from Siyeh Pass. Never did work, so we explored the head of Baring Creek. Now we climb to a notch one mile north of Goat Mountain summit and it's only a 40-minute slip-and-slide down to that bewitchingly beautiful lake. This August 1999 shot is from the notch looking west across Baring Canyon to east face of Going-to-the-Sun Mountain and Sexton glacier. Started snowing ten minutes later and lasted until we reached Rising Sun in late afternoon. No good pictures. O darn! Have to do it again.

BEST SHOT OF GRIZ TAIL—Famed Montana artist-writer Charlie Russell said, "There's no shorter grip, than a bear's tail." He learned that from a guy who actually tried. Charlie had a summer home on Lake McDonald and hung around with some very tough characters.

Facing page: FINDING A SHORTCUT—We got "cliffed out" on Mount Grinnell so I told everybody to stay put while I checked out a shortcut. Thought the goat ledge might go around to a break in the cliffs, but it didn't. Can't remember if we got down or not.

Previous pages: YE OLDE SWIMMIN' HOLE—Just about every time The Gang visits Iceberg Lake, we see young people taking a dip. They're mainly boys trying to get dates with the girls who work at Many Glacier.

WYATT THE WADER—On his first hike with Grandpa, three-year-old Wyatt splashed in Lake Josephine. We'd seen a black bear from the boat so when we got to the upper end, I handed him small binoculars to spot more bears. Ten seconds later he was looking under water with the glasses. Told me he saw a whale in there. Wyatt belongs to daughter Wendy and husband Shawn Price.

ST. MARY FALLS—The river approaches the lake in spectacular noisy fashion. It is a nice place to picnic and if your talkative aunt is along, you can't hear a word she's saying. Only about a mile from the road.

RIGHT-OF-WAY PROBLEM—Lawyer Ted is quoting federal statutes regarding "right of way" to Billy Goat. Billy disagreed so Ted found another route up cliff on Mount Piegan. This was day Dean Jellison broke his leg and didn't know it until he got home. Stepped wrong on a loose rock and hobbled down with others helping.

GLAZED CRAGS—Late September can produce some glittering frosts on the Continental Divide. Towering crags north of Gem Glacier are unnamed. We've thought about trying to climb 'em but are too busy.

Facing page: JULY CORNICES—Winter winds pile tons of snow on the lee side of Glacier's peaks and ridges. Walking out on them causes deaths of a few big animals and unwary mountaineers. Falling cornices can trigger avalanches in winter and spring. Behind Bob and Marvin is the tip of Mount St. Nicholas, 25 miles to the south.

Above: INDIAN PAINTBRUSH—Eight species of *Castilleja*, Indian paintbrush, grow in the park and it takes a doctor of botany to tell 'em apart; however, I know common paintbrush from this rare kind, Rhexia-leaved paintbrush. One of the first flowers to appear and the last to leave, paintbrush are my favorites. Always cheerful and everywhere.

Left: "THE WALL" AT AHERN—Terminus of Dr. Edwards' Pinnacle Wall goat trail to Ahern Pass shows well over Doc's right shoulder. Many have asked what Ahern Pass looks like. That's it, where the snow lies. Do not know how Lieutenant George Ahern made it up through there from Belly River valley with black cavalry troopers of the 25th Infantry in 1890, horses and all. Also had a few civilians and Indian guides. Glacier historian Jack Holterman quotes someone saying, "a route fit only for a crazy man." Holterman is kinder, calling Ahern "…a remarkably kind and courageous man…"

Right: MYSTERIOUS ROCK—Fighting our way across west ridge of Mount Ellsworth through sharp-edged boulders, we found this unusual rock. Showed it to Senator Baucus. An excuse to rest. Some believed that the pattern is petrified roots of an ancient tree. Others guessed it's lava forced into cracks by great pressure. Three voted for dinosaur do-do.

Below: THAT FEELS SO GOOD—This grizzly scratched both sides, then spent fifteen minutes working on its back. Photo taken May 6, 1999, near horse corrals at Many Glacier. You'd enjoy scratching too if you just spent five months in bed. I know guys who do it after only eight hours. Just out of hibernation, shedding of winter hair begins. A perfect scratchin' post is priceless.

Facing page: SURELY, HE'S NOT?—Bob Z. walked up to that narrow slimy log and studied it carefully, as if he might cross. You can plainly see Jack and Ray acted "ho hum," like it looked okay to them. I prepared to get pictures of disaster. Luckily Bob is a nuclear physicist, so nothing dumb happened.

ON THE HIGHEST POINT—Two guys taking each other's picture on the summit. Photo illustrates cracked composition of rock. Indian lore says some day Chief Mountain will be gone because of constant breaking up. I will not climb it again because of back trouble...yellow streak up center. The Glacier Mountaineers climbed it again in 1999.

Right: TOP IS THAT WAY—All climbing groups need someone who knows which way is up and is always eager to share this knowledge. On east ridge of Edwards Mountain, Sperry Glacier below and Little Matterhorn to the north. *(Photo of Ostrom by Walter Bahr)*

Below: FLOWER EATERS—All the split-hooved animals enjoy a tasty petunia now and then, but mule deer—like these young bucks in velvet horns—eat 'em all summer. Garden Wall above Highline Trail.

CHECK HIS DRIVER'S LICENSE—Returning from climb on Garden Wall, the Gang found this situation. We've all heard reports of bears getting into cars but this was the first we knew of one learning to drive. Notice Ivan and Elmer have their bear spray handy. Close scrutiny revealed bear was just a big teddy. He visits park with a Whitefish artist who enjoys the company.

BELLY RIVER STATION—Got this shot helicoptering into Elizabeth Lake where a grizzly had killed a lone camper in late fall of 1980. On the south sky-line is Ptarmigan Wall where trail from here goes up through tunnel to Many Glacier. Barely visible to the right is part of lofty Mount Merritt. Over-the-Hill Gang does not hike here often, but it is a magical place.

Facing page: A LAKE OF SKY—McDonald Lodge on the far shore is not clearly visible but reflections of sky certainly are. It is 4,697 vertical feet from the top of Stanton to Lake "Mac." Elmer Searle, in the middle, was still climbing in year 2000 at 81.

A BIG GRIZZLY—Son Shannon and I saw this large fellow on Mount Altyn in late May. His sighting was frosting on a day when we'd seen an even bigger one chase a young ram on Mount Henkle. Watched that drama through field glasses but it was too far for pictures. The ram had no trouble outrunning the bear and we think the big guy was just being frisky. After pursuing the bighorn a short distance, the griz ran and slid down a snow field. Did it mostly in sitting position but tried a couple of "belly flops." The bear in this photo studied me for a minute then walked off shaking his head.

Facing page: BEYOND THE CLIFFS—Goat trail on Grinnell Point completed, the Gang pauses to gaze in "childlike wonder." Mountain to the south is Allen. Lake Josephine features scenic boat rides for non-climbers.

Right: DON'T BE NERVOUS, JACK—Fletcher said this is the closest he ever got to a wild bull moose. One time here a big bull lay down in dense brush before we could get a picture. Stood around for an hour and he didn't move. I yelled to Bob, "If I rolled a rock in there he'd probably stand up." Right then three lady hikers came 'round the bend and one said, "George! You roll a rock in there and I'll tell the rangers." Didn't know who she was, but told her I was just kiddin'.

Below: WHERE LOGAN CREEK STARTS— Everyone can enjoy October colors here. Park Service built a handicapped walkway at Oberlin Bend and I shot this over the railing.

PRACTICAL JOKER—Every time we descend this cut in the cliffs at Comeau Pass, Vern perches up there and throws snow on those passing below. We believe it is hangover from his career in the military. Akaiyan and Feather Woman lakes lie to the south.

STANTON AND VAUGHT—Winter view of the scenic peaks northeast of Lake McDonald. The big lake freezes over every few years. Glacier Mountaineers Club tried to start a tradition of climbing Stanton each New Year's Eve. That did not prove wildly popular, but we all love it in the summer.

Facing page: WATCHING THE CLOUDS ROLL IN—View west up St. Mary is always intoxicating and clouds add mystic quality. Later that afternoon, too much mystique drove us off Otokomi Mountain. Big peaks are Little Chief, Dusty Star, and Citadel with Gunsight Pass on horizon.

DAWN AT MANY GLACIER—Grinnell Point can be any color it chooses. Took pic just after summer sunrise from the hotel. Decided to climb it again.

THE SENATOR INCIDENT—
Montana's senior U.S. Senator, Max Baucus, will not forget this day. That's him, second from the left…before "the incident." Ivan and Walter said it would be a fifteen-mile "pleasure stroll" from Lubec to Firebrand then DeSanto Pass, down Buttercup Park, and out to Two Medicine. First seven miles were great but the middle was bad.

Late in the day at Paradise Creek, we stopped to wash cuts and scrapes. Safety pin on Baucus' bear spray was lost, so sitting caused elbow to trigger smelly choking gas all over his body. He did not say one bad word, even after he could talk again.

Later, at Elmer's van, everyone began choking and coughing when Max got in. All agreed it wouldn't look good driving out of Glacier Park with a U.S. Senator tied to the roof rack. Put him in the rear seat, opened all windows and drove fast.

A SHORT TROUBLED LIFE—
Met this grizzly and cub in October 1995 during a close encounter of the uptight kind. Named her Tillie but bear managers called her "The Lake Five Bear." She came out of the Park in 1995 where her female cub was killed by a train. She and male cub were transplanted deep into Glacier, where I got this picture. That cub was eventually shot near a home in Coram. Tillie had no cubs in 1997 but did in '98. One of those cubs was probably killed by another bear in early summer. I photographed Tillie and the remaining cub near Sprague Creek in late summer. Something happened to the cub after that. It wasn't seen again. Flew check flight with biologist in fall of '99 and Tillie's radio collar showed her near Lake McDonald. She hibernated on nearby Glacier Wall. Came out in spring of 2000 and hiked for forty minutes with the Over-the-Hill Gang on the Boundary Trail Thursday, April 20. Tillie was illegally shot the following weekend at Lake Five just west of the park by a young bear hunter who mistook her for a legal black bear. She was twelve years old.

Left: BALSAMROOT—A springtime flower that blooms by the millions on sunny slopes at middle elevations. Most big game animals like to eat the young plants.

Right: FOR THE HANDICAPPED—There are three wheelchair trails now in Glacier, at Oberlin Bend near Logan Pass, another at Pitamakan Falls near Two Medicine, and this one, Trail of the Cedars, at Avalanche. The creek roaring down from Avalanche Lake has cut a colorful gorge through the rocks and standard books about Glacier have this view from the bridge. No reason this book should be completely different.

Facing page: LISTENING TO WATERFALLS—Avalanche Lake is fed by melt from Sperry Glacier and surrounding mountains. Peak in distance is Gunsight. Two-mile hike in here is so popular there is a biffy. From high on cliffs south of the lake, we have counted eighteen waterfalls.

A STARRY RILL—Of all Glacier's wonders, water intrigues me most. Friendly clouds and angry storms from half the world journey here to unload their gatherings, so great rivers may ever flow to three oceans. In the driest of seasons, Glacier remains an amazing land of ice, ponds, lakes, and streams. Jack Fletcher is good at rill shots so we put one here. *(Fletcher photo)*

COLORS THAT FLUTTER—Sunlight shining through wings of a monarch butterfly remind me of stained glass. Monarch and swallowtail friend were up to something on a river bank. Hope it was proper.

Facing Page: NORTH RIDGE ROUTE—Clouds rolled in as we negotiated a tricky ledge far above Bird Woman Cirque on an August climb of Clements. We made the summit in fine shape. A lone climber fell here in early 1999 and recovering his body was a major operation. Do not climb alone and never do this ledge if there is even a trace of snow or ice.

FROM THE NORTH—Early autumn picture of Chief Mountain from due north along road to Waterton shows where last great rockfall took place in early 1990s. Million tons fell from north face just to the right of its center. Note lighter area.

Left: ST. MARY VALLEY WITH POND—Highway 89 was rebuilt in 1999 and it goes closer to this little pond south of St. Mary. Farthest peaks are Gunsight and Fusillade, deep inside the park. Photo was taken September 24.

Below: CLIMBING THROUGH COLORS—Glacier Park is noted for color, every hue and tint of the spectrum is here. Billiant or subdued, color is in trees, rocks, mosses, lichens, flowers, birds, and beasts…gaudy bright splashes or tiny dots of brilliance. Come fall and the dazzle is foliage, from dwarf willow to large alders, mountain ash, larch, and aspen. We had fourteen miles of foliage display on September hike to a lake below Red Mountain. Bob Z. figured this was an excellent spot for contemplation of nature and the meaning of life.

LOST KID—Ever see a small child lose his mother (below) in a supermarket? Same thing here. This newborn kid wanted to nurse and mother nosed him back so he ran away. Returned in five minutes but mother had gone to water. He couldn't find her. Pure panic. Desperate little guy ran helter skelter bleating distress. This shot caught all four feet off the ground as he checked everywhere. I'm sure his mother could hear but was teaching him a lesson. Kid found her and they headed into the cliffs. Life is good.

Facing page: OUT ON "THE WALL"—Gordon Edwards, upper right of center, is catching up to Gang members. He'd stopped to show three smarter ones an escape notch back over the Ptarmigan Wall rather than crossing here to Ahern pass. I put away the camera for remainder of this crossing and took no pictures coming back. Gordon told us if we fell, there was enough air-time for the Lord's Prayer.

Above: WILD CROCUS—Pasque flowers are early bloomers at lower elevation. Colors range from purple to nearly white. These are the lavenderish-pink kind.

Left: SUMMER ON THE GARDEN WALL—Ray on the Highline Trail. Continental Divide stretches southward past Haystack Butte toward Logan Pass.

Above: PEOPLE DRIVE THERE—This shot shows both Going-to-the-Sun Road and the Highline Trail as they traverse the Garden Wall north of Logan Pass. Looks slightly scary from this angle on Oberlin.

Right: EDEN AND BEYOND—Elizabeth Richardson takes in the panoramic St. Mary Valley from Reynolds summit. Eastern section of Going-to-the-Sun Road wends its way up from St. Mary Lake past Goat Mountain, Going-to-the-Sun, and Matahpi. The sharp ridge of Heavy Runner lies below. Right of that is our beloved hanging valley of Eden. Peaks at right are Dusty Star, Little Chief, Mahtatopa, and Red Eagle. Divide Mountain in distance.

ICEBERG LAKE—Aerial shot of Iceberg cirque, Iceberg Peak and Continental Divide, with Notch to the right and Mt. Wilbur at left. August photo with lots of bergs floating. We did see this lake completely clear one early October. You can get this same view by climbing Crowfeet Mountain, and it's cheaper.

Above: GRIZZLY IN PETUNIAS—Used a 400 MM lens to shoot this guy on Altyn. Ray and I saw him above the Iceberg Trail and darned if he didn't come down. It was not a deliberate approach, just feeding our way. A group of hikers didn't see him in brush fifty feet from them. Not finding berries, he went back up the sidehill digging roots. Approximately eighty percent of Glacier grizzly diet is vegetation. Not so with big cousins in Alaska's salmon country.

Below: BEARGRASS SLOPE—Some years, those big plants completely dominate the scenery in places. These on Going-to-the-Sun Mountain in early August.

SHOULD BE PATAKI—
Remains of an old prospector
mine are still here above
Cracker Lake. This is too
beautiful a place to call
Cracker. A man who helped
create Glacier Park, James
Willard Schultz, had named
this lake after his Blackfeet
mother-in-law, Pataki, meaning Carrier Woman. The hike
in here from Many Glacier is
through notorious grizzly
country. An injury attack in
recent years was on a mid-
west couple and embarrass-
ment ensued. "Thou shouldst
avoid griz attacks if thee
vacationeth with thy neigh-
bor's wife."

ONE MILE UP—Every step of Baring Creek trail reveals colors but this section is especially dazzling. Besides the blazing palette of rocks and lichens, there are waterfalls and flowers. Just above here is the biggest cascade. The Over-the-Hill Gang goes there so often, we've heard of rangers calling it Viagra Falls.